The new boy had five sisters and one brother.
His sisters were all older than him,
but his brother was a baby.
The new boy, his sisters and his brother
lived in a big, new house
with their father and mother.

2

The new boy's house was near the road.
Many people came and looked at the house
because it was so big and new.
When the children ran past
they stopped and looked at it.
When the bus drove past
the driver stopped and looked at it.
When the people walked past
they stopped and looked at it.
They came in the morning, in the afternoon,
and at night. They all liked the house.

The new boy and his sisters liked it too.
"We live in the best house,"
said the new boy to his sisters.
"Our house is better than the other houses."

4

The new boy's house was big and new,
but the yard was very dirty.
There were big stones and old tins in the yard.
The trees were old, and goats ran round.
There were no flowers at all.
Behind the house there was a storm drain
which had dirty water in it.

One day the new boy's mother said,
"Your brother cannot play in this yard.
He could have an accident here.
He could cut his hands on the old tins.
If he fell in the storm drain
he could not get out.
Children, it is time for school now,
but after school you must all help me.
You must clean up the yard.
I will tell you what to do."

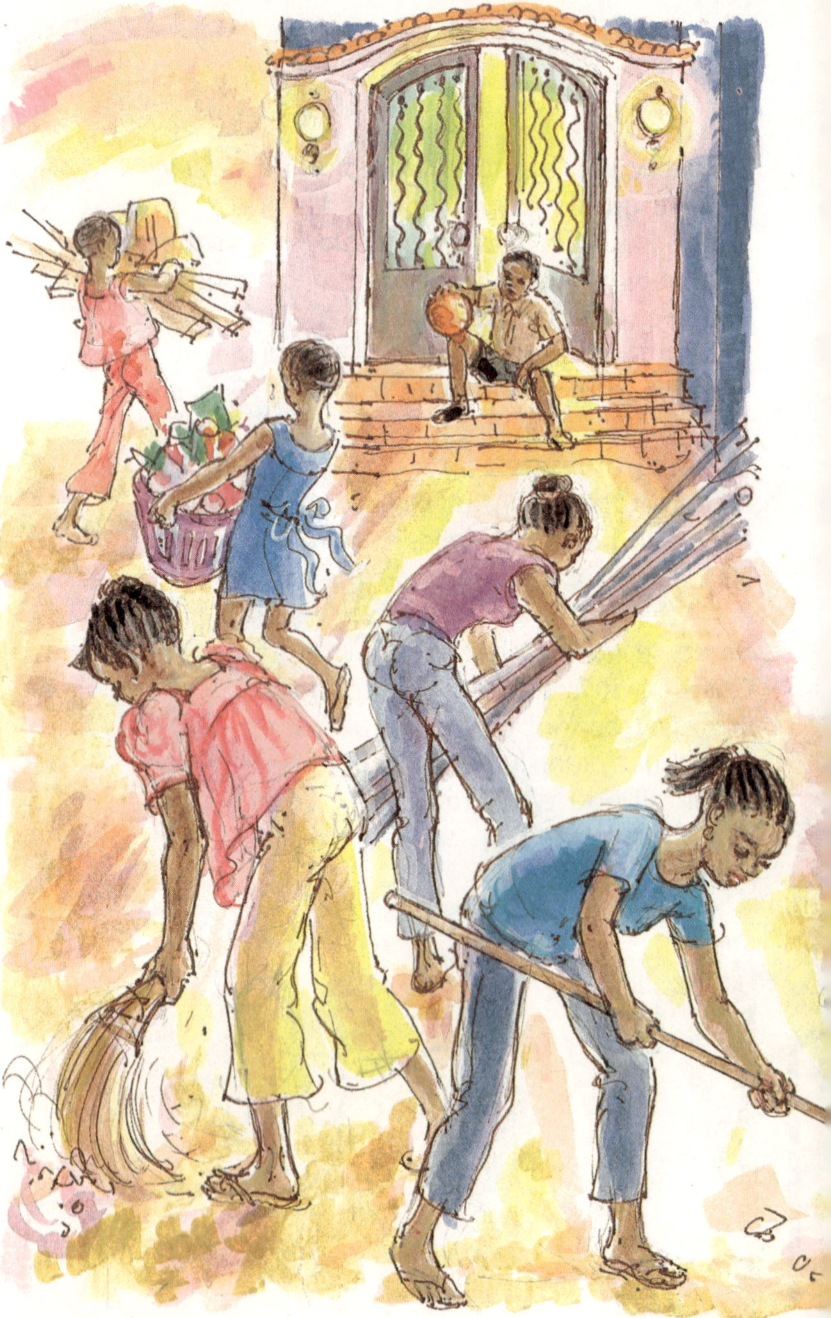

The five sisters were all tired after school,
but every day they ran home and helped.
"First tie up the goats," said their mother.
"Then cut down the broken trees,
and then clean up the yard."

The new boy did not help at all.
He did not like helping his sisters,
so he did not come home after school.
He played football in the school yard.
He liked all sports, but he liked football best.
He wanted to practise and be in the team.
He practised every day after school.
He came home when it was night,
and he did not help his sisters at all.

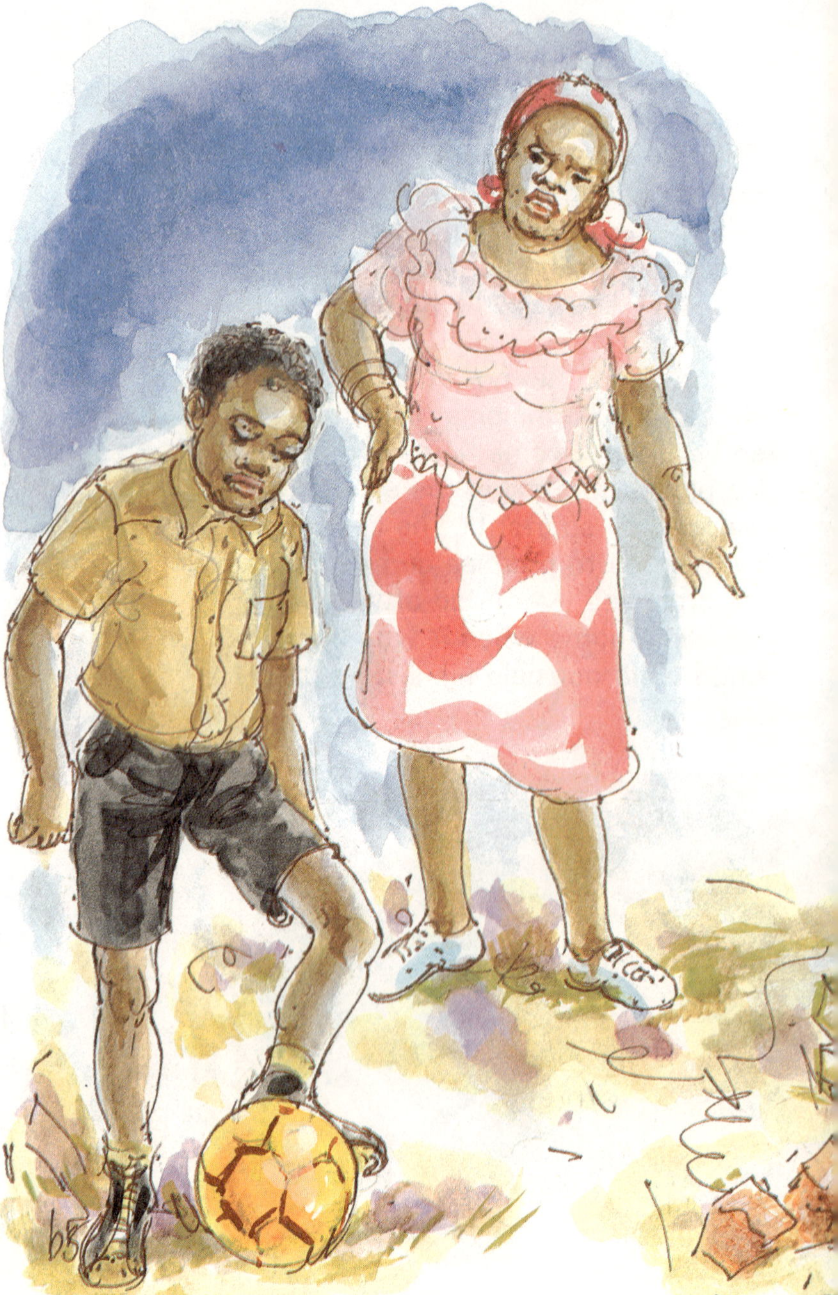

When the new boy came home on Friday night
his mother was angry with him.
"Your sisters helped every day after school,
but you did not help at all," she said.
"You did not help on Monday or Tuesday
or Wednesday or Thursday or today.
Tomorrow is Saturday.
You do not go to school on Saturday or Sunday,
so you can help me then.
I will tell you what to do now.
First you must throw away all the old tins,
and then you must clean out the storm drain.
There is dirty water in the storm drain
and you must clean it out.
Now do not forget.
First you must throw away all the old tins,
and then you must clean out the storm drain."

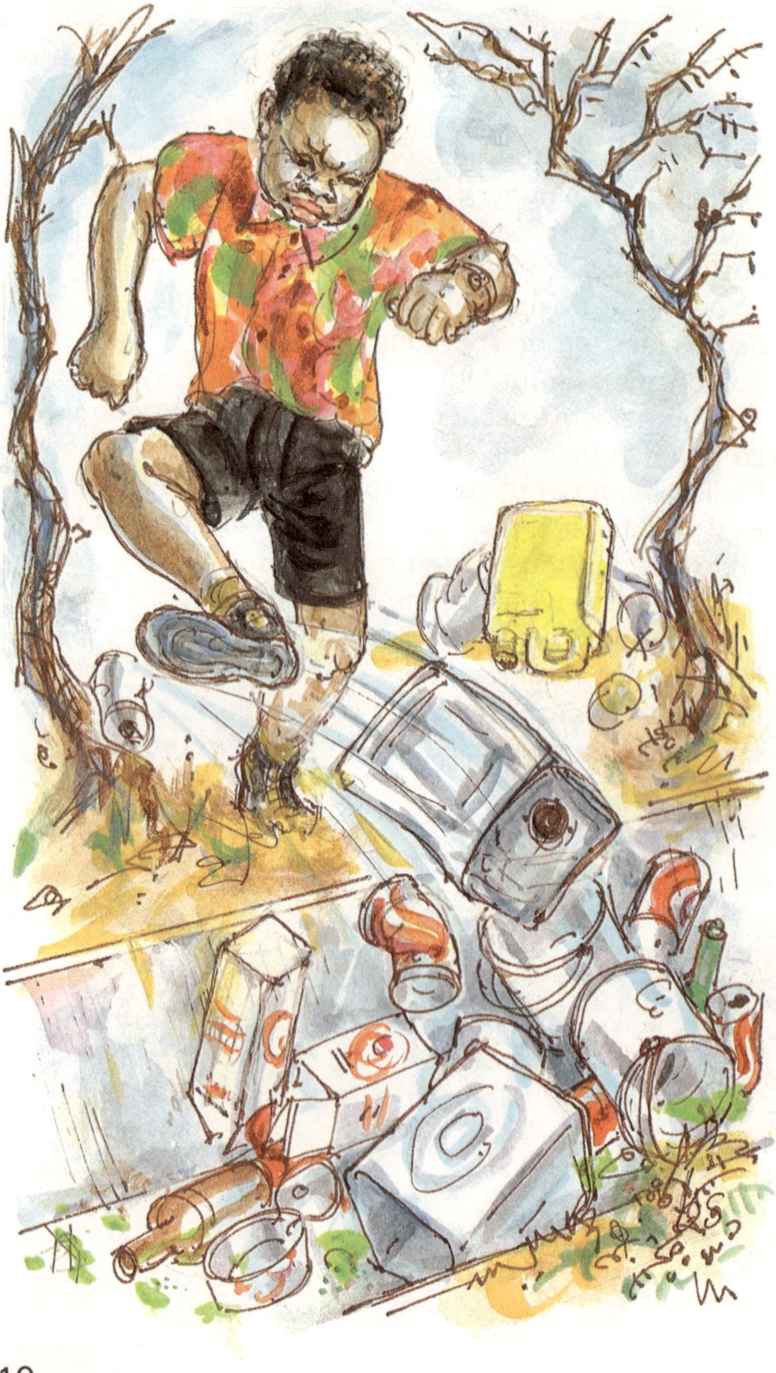

But the new boy did not help on Saturday.
His mother took his sisters to the market,
and the new boy walked out into the yard.
He looked round. He did not want to help.
"I am not going to clean out the storm drain.
I will throw the old tins in the storm drain,
and then I will practise for the team," he said.

So that is what he did.
First he threw the old tins in the storm drain.
Then he kicked his football round the yard.
Then he talked to some people who walked past.
Then he ran races in the road.
Then he was hot and tired,
and he wanted some water,
so he sat down near the house.

When his mother came home he was asleep.
"Did you clean out the storm drain?
Did you throw the tins away?" she asked.
"Yes, Mother, I did," said the new boy.
"I am so hot. I want some cold water.
Is it time for food now?"
The new boy did not help at all,
but his mother did not know.

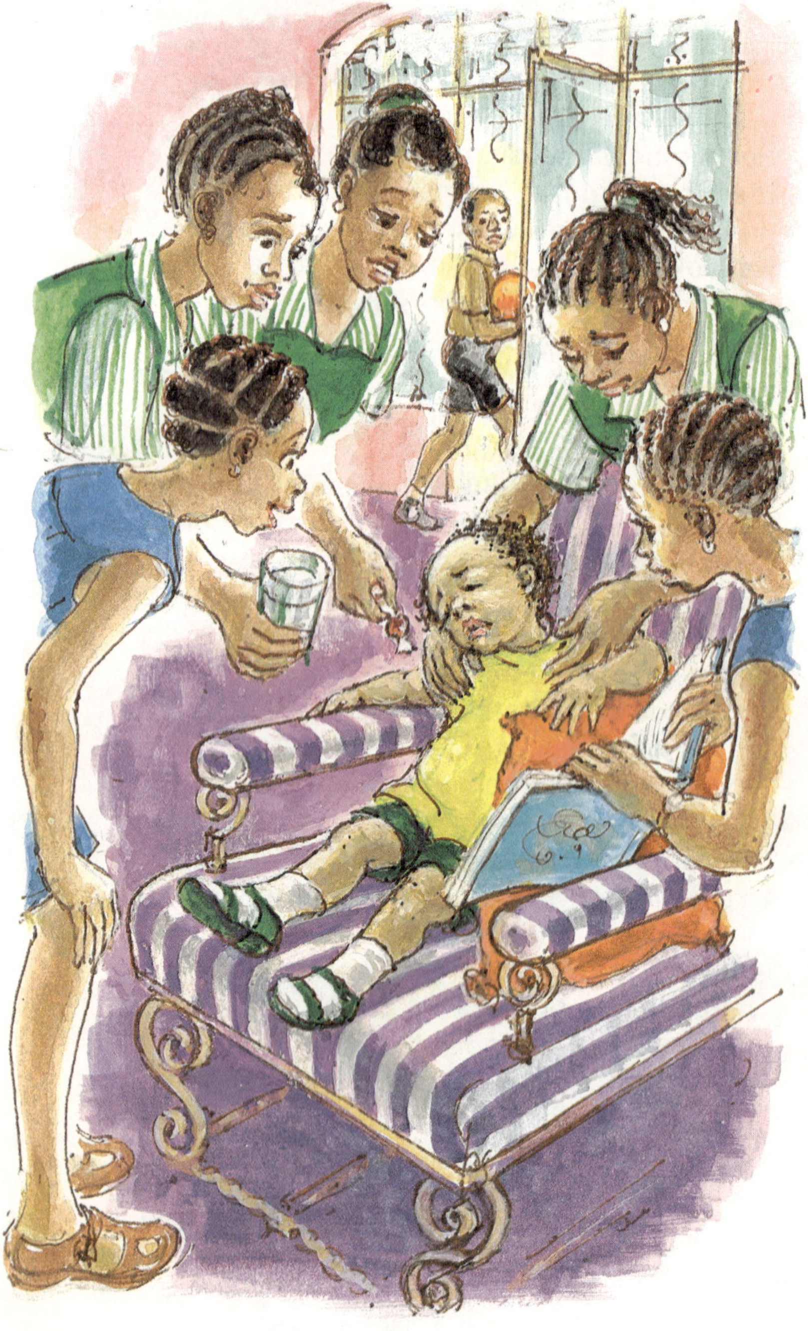

After that the new boy's mother forgot
the old tins and the dirty storm drain.

One day the baby did not want to play.
He sat very still in a chair.
He was very, very tired.
His five sisters knew that he was not happy.
"What do you want?" they asked.
"Do you want some cold water?"
"Do you want a sweet?"
"Do you want to play in the yard?"
"Do you want to look at a book?"

The baby did not want water or a sweet.
He did not want to sit up or play.
He was ill, but he could not tell them.
His sisters said, "Go to bed now,
and you will be better tomorrow.
You will be better in the morning."

The new boy did not talk to his brother.
He said, "I am going out to play.
I do not want to sit in the house all day."

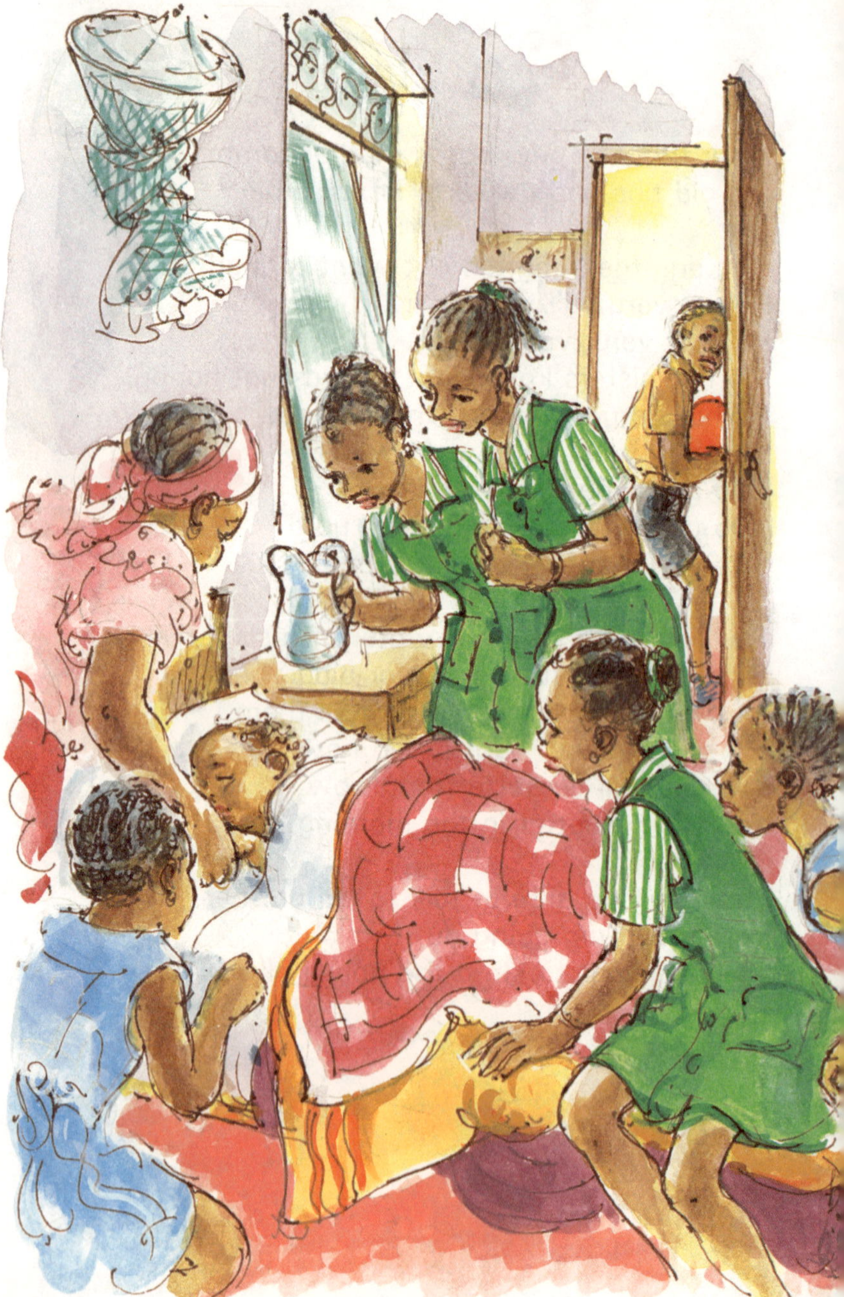

The baby was not better in the morning.
He was very cold, and his legs hurt.
He did not want his food, and he was tired.
His mother knew that he was ill.
He was very still. His mother talked to him.
"You will get better," she said.
"Give me your hand. You are so cold.
Do you want some water?
There is cold water in this jug. It is for you."

The five sisters wanted to help their brother.
They touched his head. It was very cold.
"He is so cold and still. Is he ill?
What can we do for him?" they asked.

The new boy did not want to help.
He said, "I must go and practise
because I want to be in the team."

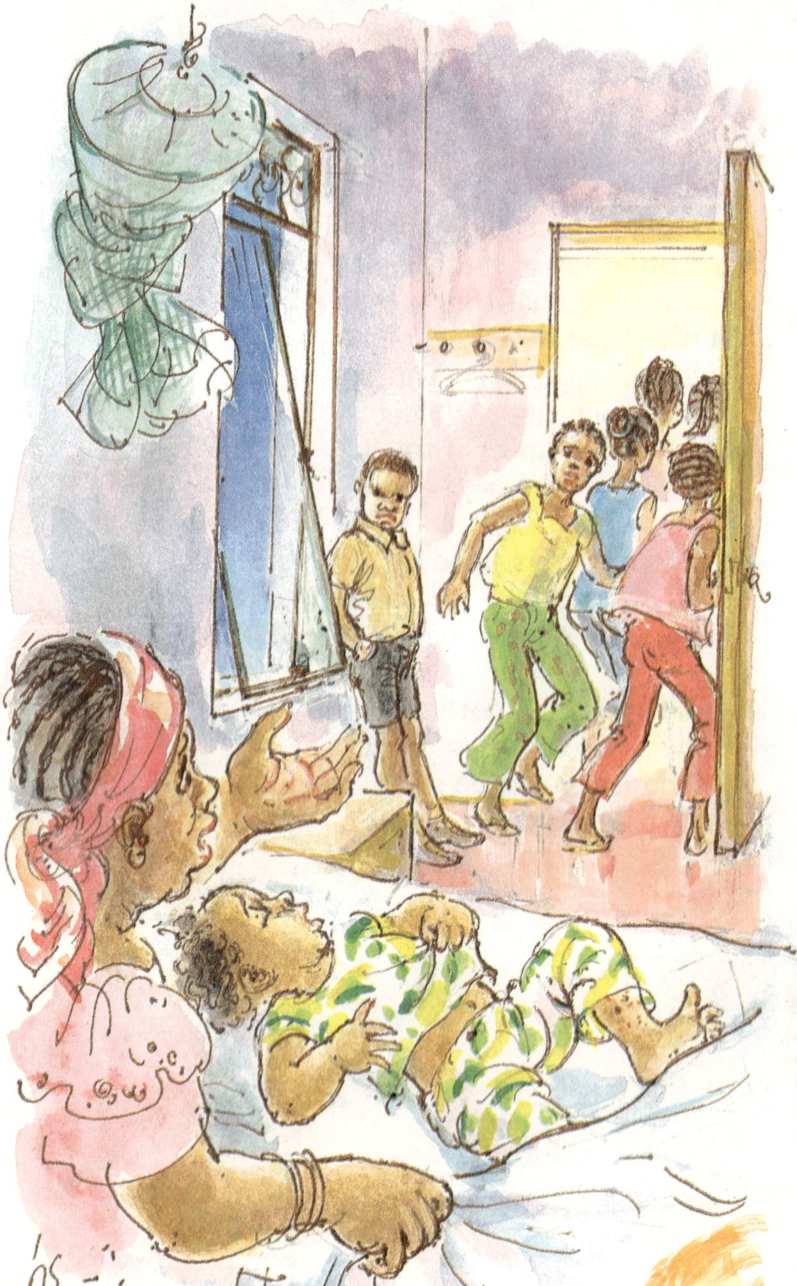

The baby did not get better,
and that night he was very ill.
When his mother touched him he was not cold.
He was very hot, and his head hurt too.
He did not want food or water.
His mother sat with him and talked to him.
She knew that he was very ill.

At last she said, "The doctor must come.
Girls, run to the hospital as fast as you can.
Tell the doctor that your brother is ill.
Ask her to come to the baby.
The doctor will know what to do."
The five sisters ran to the hospital.
They ran as fast as they could.

The new boy did not go with them. He said,
"I am the best runner. I can run races,
but I am not going to run now.
I am too tired. I want my food."

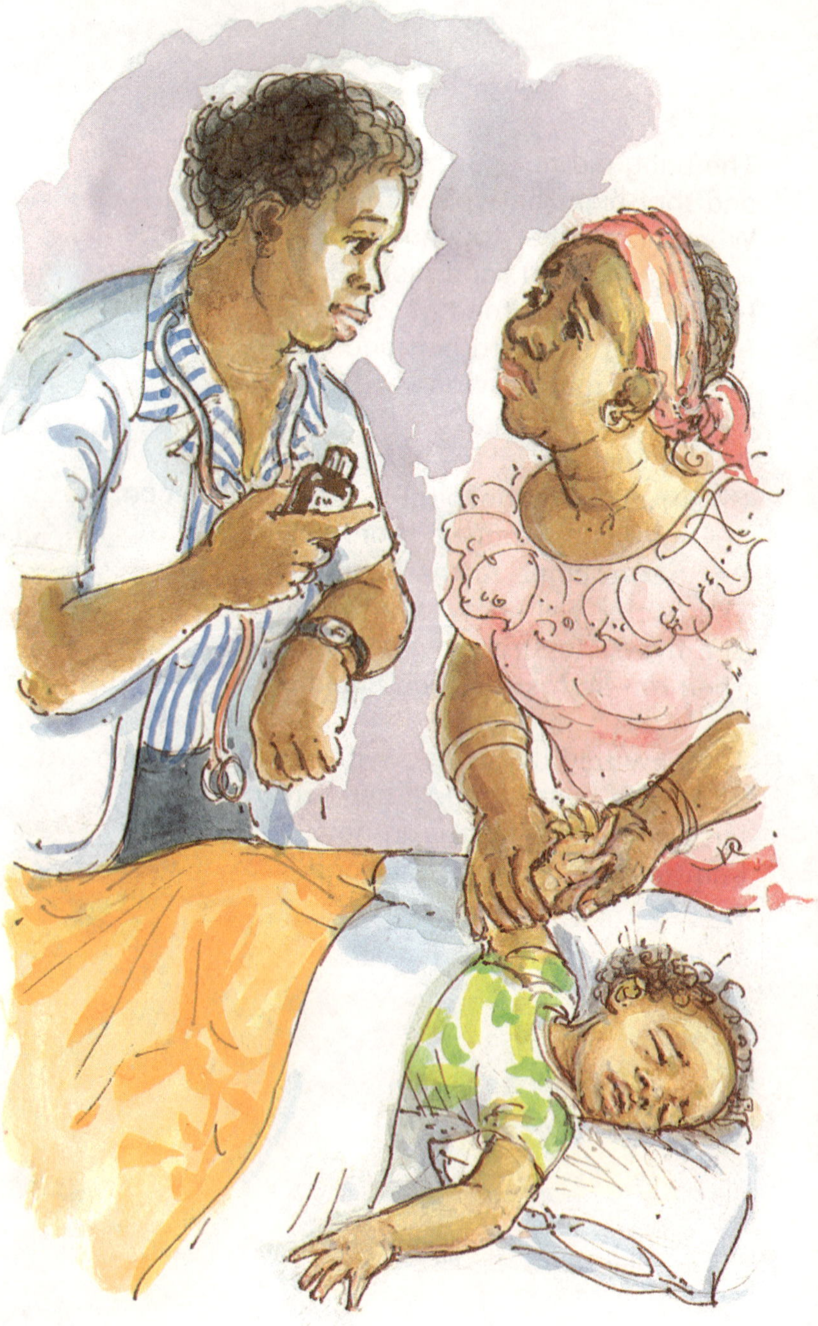

The doctor came to see the baby.
She looked at him. She touched his hand.
The baby was very, very ill.
"Doctor, please help him," said his mother.
"Yesterday he was tired,
and he did not want to play.
This morning he was cold.
He did not want food or water.
Now he is very hot, and his head hurts.
Is he very ill?"

The doctor said, "Yes, he is very ill.
He has malaria, but I can help him.
I will give him some pills to stop malaria.
What time is it now? Ten o'clock?
I will give him one pill now.
Then you must give him a second pill
at two o'clock in the morning.
Then you must give him a third pill
at six o'clock in the morning.
Give him some water when he takes the pills.
Do not forget. He must take the pills.
I am going home now,
but I will come at ten o'clock tomorrow."

20

The baby's mother sat with him all night.
The baby took the second pill at two o'clock,
and the third pill at six o'clock.
When the doctor came at ten o'clock she asked,
"How is he today? Is he better?"
The baby's mother said, "He took the pills,
but he is very hot and his head hurts."

The doctor looked at the baby. Then she said,
"This is not good. He is very ill,
and malaria can kill children.
The pills will help him,
and you must give him water too.
I am going to give him a pill now.
If he is not better this afternoon
I will take him to the hospital."

The five sisters sat with their baby brother.
The new boy threw stones at dogs in the road.

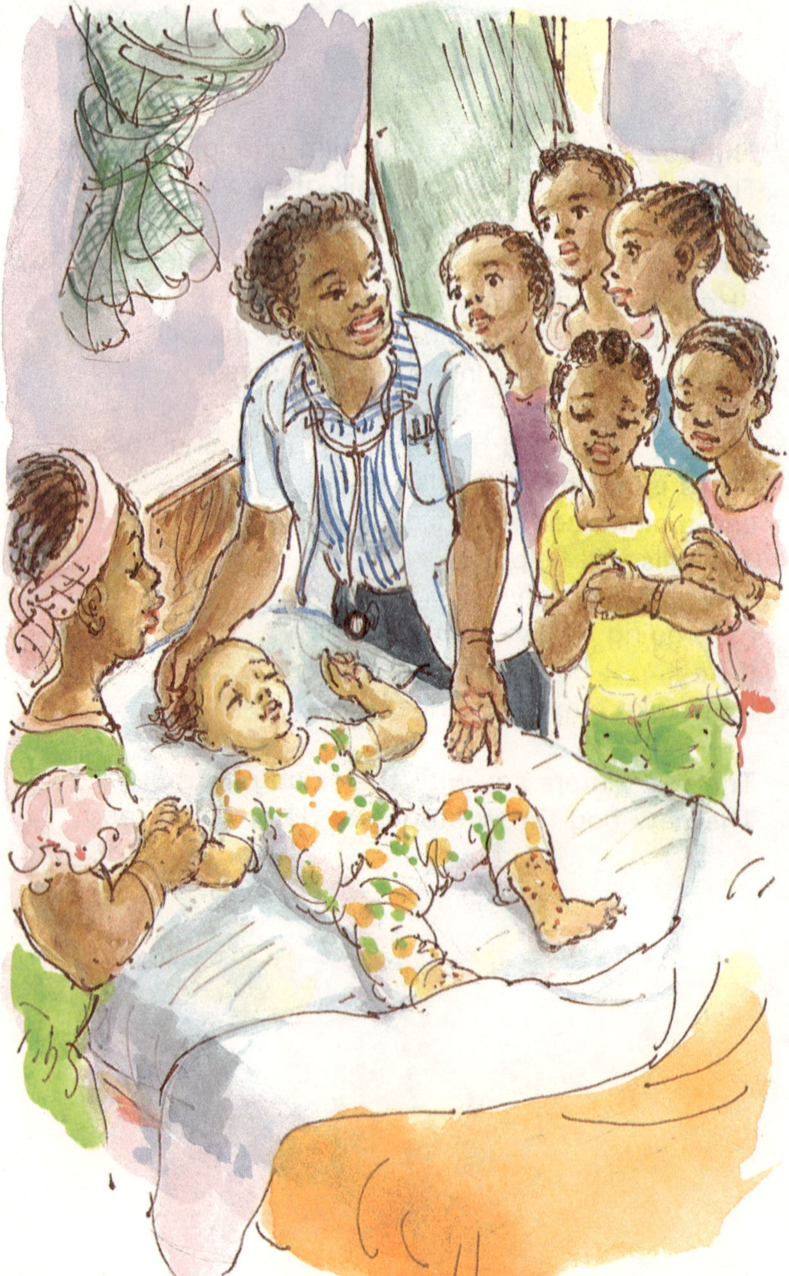

When the doctor came in the afternoon
the baby was asleep, and he was not so hot.
The doctor put her hand on the baby's head.
"Your brother is better," she said to the girls.
"The malaria is going away."
The baby's mother was very happy.
"Doctor, thank you, thank you," she said.

The five sisters were happy too,
but they did not know what malaria was.
"Doctor, what is malaria?" they asked.
"How did our brother get malaria?"

"A mosquito bit him," said the doctor.
"If a mosquito bites you
it can give you malaria.
Look at your brother's legs.
He has many mosquito bites on his legs.
He has malaria and he is so ill
because a mosquito bit him.
All mosquito bites hurt,
but some can give you malaria."

24

"If I see a mosquito, I will kill it,"
said one of the sisters.
"That is good," said the doctor.
"But there are other things that you can do.
Malaria kills many people,
but you children can help to stop it."
"What can we do?" the sisters asked.

"I will tell you," said the doctor.
"Mosquitoes bite you at night.
They bite you when you are asleep in bed,
or playing in the house.
If you shut all the doors and windows,
the mosquitoes cannot come into the house,
and they cannot bite you.
So shut all the doors and windows at night.
Walk around the house
and shut all the doors and windows.
Then the mosquitoes cannot come in and bite you.
That will help to stop malaria."

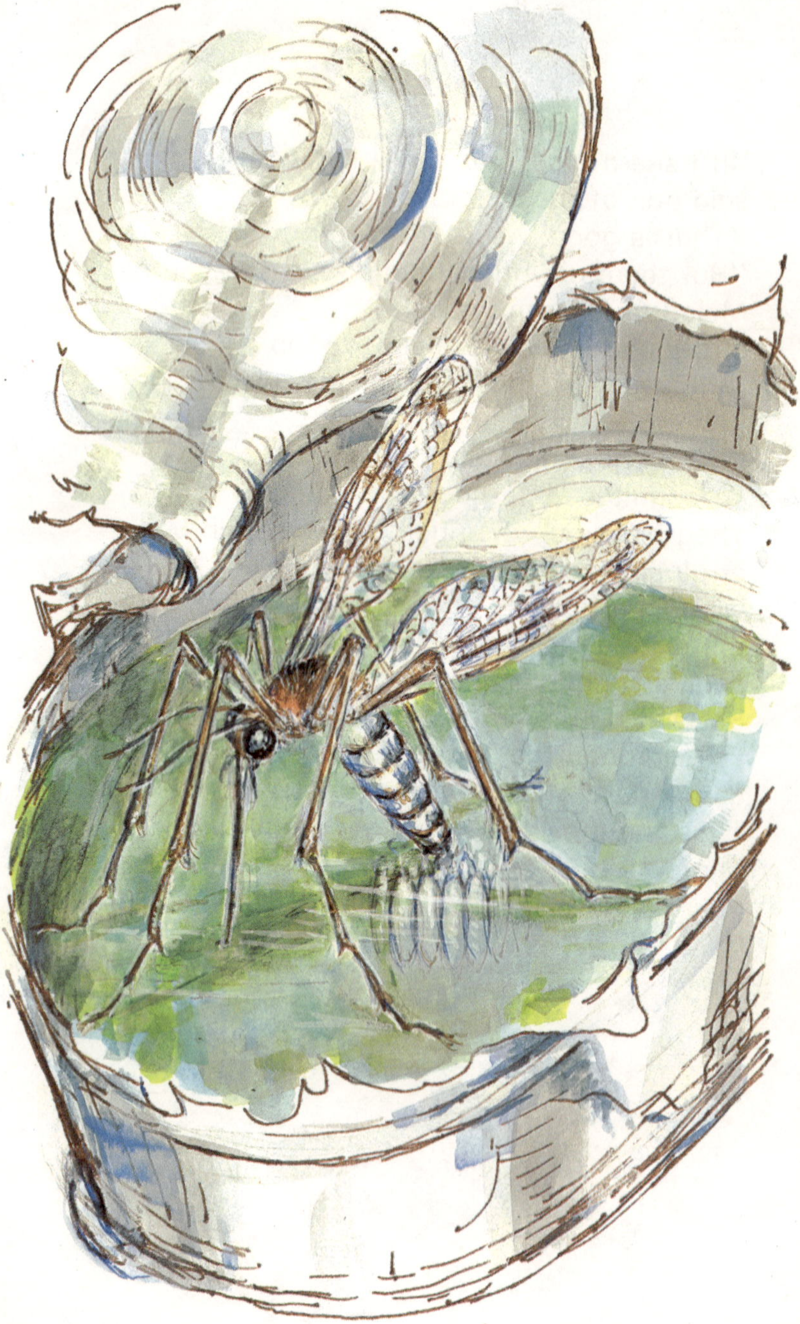

"Where do mosquitoes live?" asked the sisters.
"Mosquitoes live near water," said the doctor.
"There is no water here," said the sisters.
"There is a river near the school,
but there is no water near this house."

"Mosquitoes do not like that river.
The water in that river is too fast.
Mosquitoes like still, dirty water best.
If there is still, dirty water,
the mosquitoes will live near it.
You must look round your yard.
If there is one small tin,
and it has dirty water in it,
mosquitoes will live there.
Go and look round your yard now.
Look behind the trees and near the road.
If there is still, dirty water in the yard,
you must throw it away," said the doctor.

The new boy's mother said,
"I know that there is no dirty water here
because the children cleaned up the yard,
but we will look. Doctor, please come too."

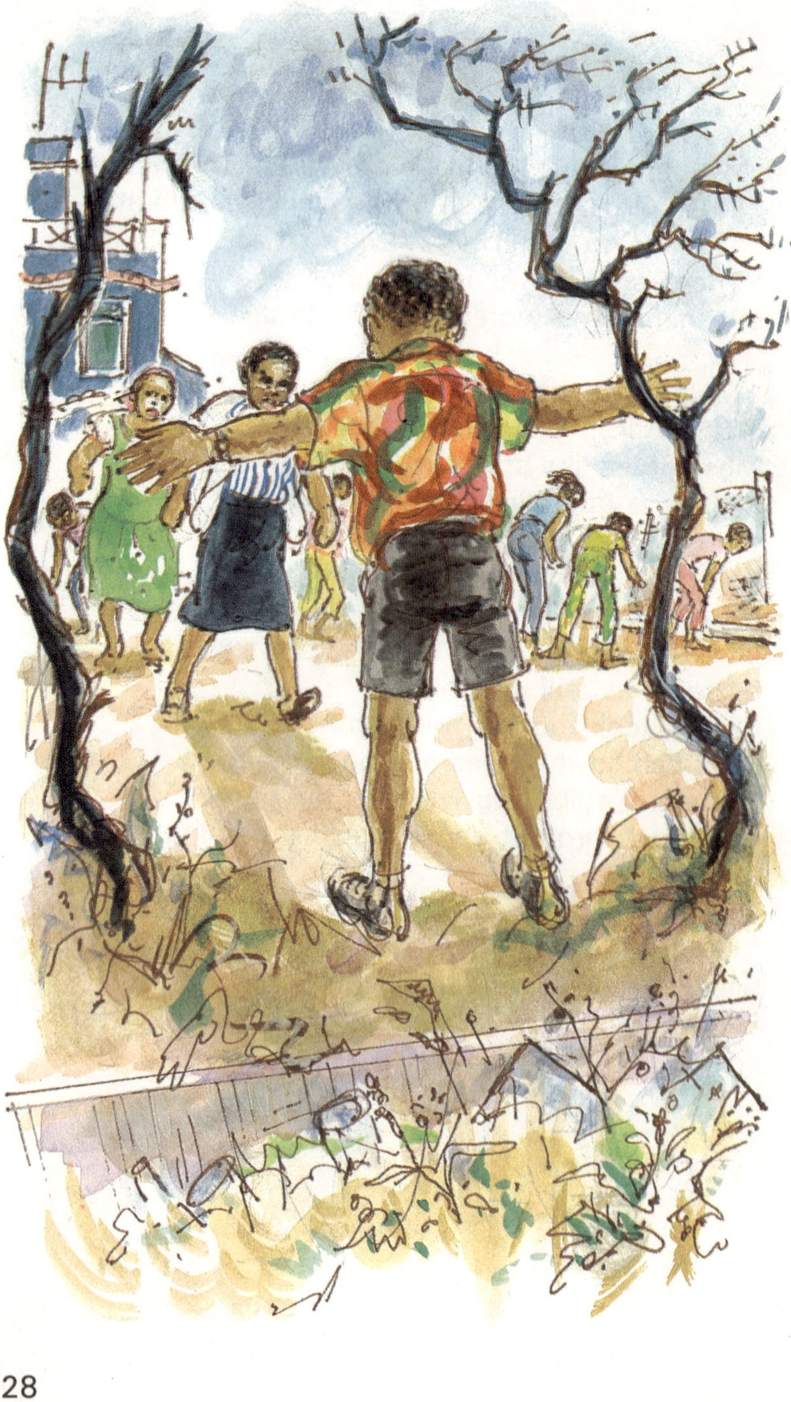

They all walked round the yard,
but there was no still, dirty water.
At last the doctor said,
"There are no mosquitoes in your yard,
but before we go into the house
we must look behind the trees."

"I will do that," said the new boy.
"You go in. I will look behind the trees."
"No, we will all look," said the doctor.
"But you are so tired," said the new boy.
"I tell you, there is no water there."

"There is a storm drain, but it is clean,"
said the new boy's mother.
"Yes, I cleaned it out," said the new boy.
"There is no water in the storm drain.
Can we go into the house now?
There is no water in our yard."

"We are very near to the storm drain
so we will look at it," said the doctor.
She walked past the new boy,
and looked into the storm drain.

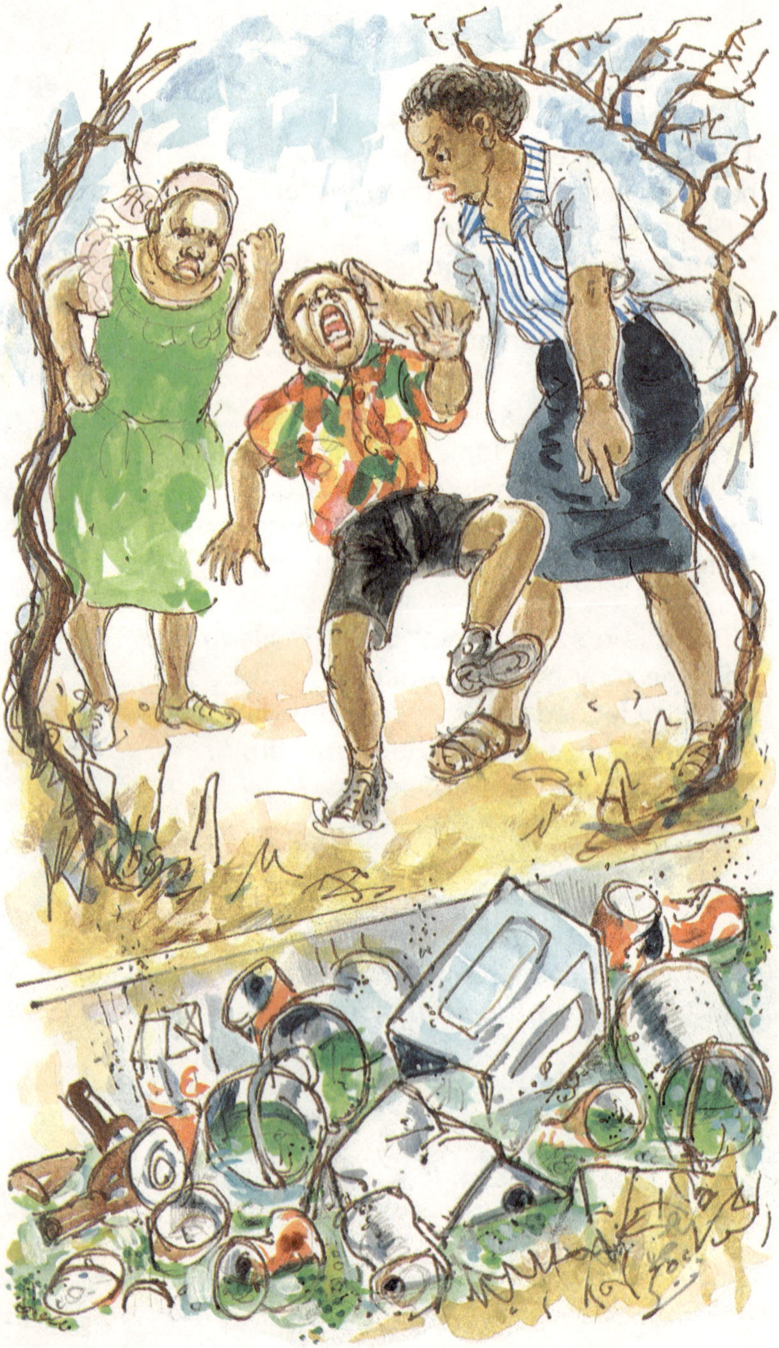

"What is this? Who did this?" asked the doctor.
The new boy's mother and his sisters
were behind the doctor.
"What?" they asked. "Who did what?"

The doctor was very angry. She said,
"Who threw the old tins into the storm drain?
There is dirty water in the storm drain,
and dirty water in the tins too.
This is where the mosquitoes live.
The baby is ill because of this.
He has malaria because of the mosquitoes,
and they live in this dirty storm drain.
Who threw the old tins in the storm drain?"

The new boy's mother knew who did it.
She knew who threw the tins in the storm drain,
and she was very angry too.
"You did this," she said to the new boy.
"You threw the old tins into the storm drain.
Your brother is ill because of you.
The mosquitoes in this storm drain bit him,
and now he has malaria. He is very, very ill."

The new boy was afraid. He wanted to run away,
but his mother said, "Go to your father.
He will know what to do with you."

The new boy's father did know what to do.
"When your mother tells you what to do,
then you must do it," he said.
"You must not play football or run races.
You must not practise for the sports team.
You must help your mother and your sisters.
Clean out the storm drain
and throw the old tins away now."